# Contents

Any words appearing in the text in bold, **like this**, are explained in the glossary.

# What Are Materials?

The word "material" is often used to mean cloth. Scientists use the word differently. To scientists, "material" means anything that things are made of.

plastic

metal

rubber

This bicycle is made of more than one material. Some things are made of one main material. This book you are reading is made mostly of paper.

# Where Do Materials Come From?

Materials are either **natural** or **synthetic**. Natural materials come from plants or animals, or they are found in the ground.

Everything in this picture is a natural material.

People make synthetic materials from oil. Plastic and nylon are two kinds of synthetic materials. Some synthetic materials can look like natural ones.

# Wood

Wood is a **natural** material. It comes from trees. Some trees are grown to be cut down. They are used to make many different things.

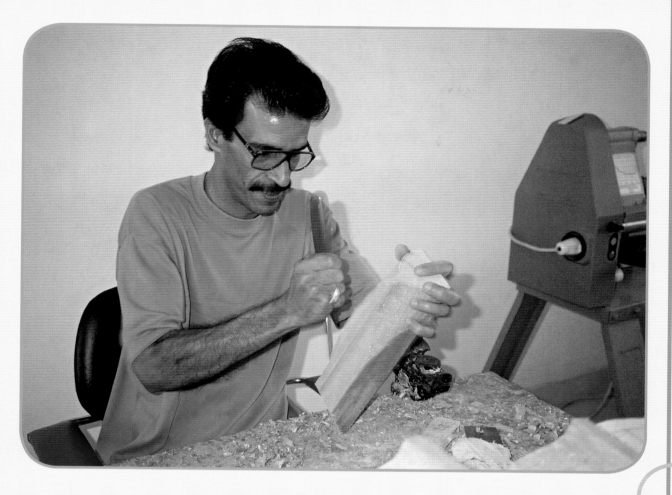

It is easy to cut wood into different shapes.
Wood is strong, and it is not as heavy as
stone and many metals.

# Paper

To make paper, wood is shredded into very small pieces. It is then mashed with water to make a **pulp**. This is spread into a thin layer. When it dries, it becomes sheets of paper.

Paper is used for many things. You can write on paper and color it with ink or paint. Paper is folded to make books, magazines, and bags.

# Materials from Animals

Sheep have thick, woolly coats. The wool is shaved off and **spun** into balls of wool. This woman is spinning. Her hat has been **knitted** from wool.

After cows die, their skin can be made into leather. This pony's saddle and bridle are made of leather.

bridle

saddle

# Rock and Stone

Rocks and stones are strong and hard. They are used to build houses and other things. This house is made of stone and so is the roof.

Some stones are **rare** and very pretty. When they are **polished**, they sparkle. Rubies are red. What color are sapphires? (Answer on page 31.)

sapphire

pearl

diamond

ruby

# Clay

Clay is a kind of mud. When it is soft, you can make it into any shape. Then it is baked hard and dried in a hot oven called a kiln.

All of these things are made of materials that come from the ground.

Bricks are made from thick blocks of clay. China is made from thin pieces of clay. It breaks easily.

# Glass

Glass is made mainly from sand. The sand is heated in a very hot fire until it melts. This man is blowing the **molten** glass into shape.

Most glass is transparent. This means you can see through it. Some glass is colored and you cannot see through it.

# Metals

Metals are found in rocks in the ground. This gold miner is breaking up rock that has gold in it. Gold and silver are **precious** metals.

This airplane is made of aluminum.

Most metals are hard, shiny, and strong. Steel and aluminum are two metals that are used to make machines.

# Rusting and Rotting

Unless it is **treated**, iron slowly rusts. It turns brown and crumbles. Wood slowly **rots** if it is left outside in the damp air.

Iron and wood are often covered with paint to stop them from rusting and rotting. The paint on this ship keeps the water, rain, and damp air out.

# Plastic

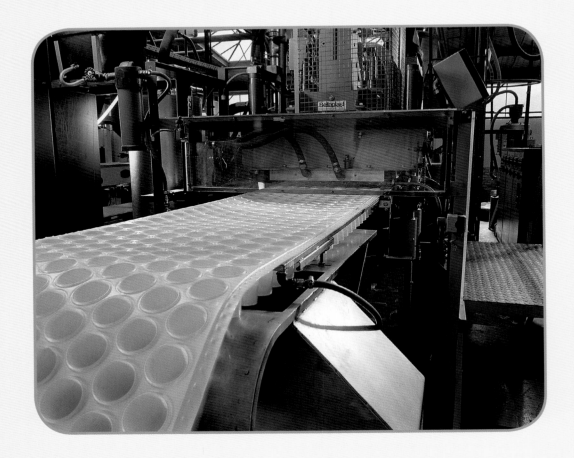

Plastic is made in a factory. Hot, runny plastic is poured into **molds** to make any kind of shape. Plastic is cheap, light, and **waterproof**.

Some plastic is hard but some is soft and **flexible**. Which of the things in the picture can be bent or folded? (Answer on page 31.)

# Clothes

Cotton comes from a plant. It is a **natural** material. Polyester, rayon, and nylon are made from oil. They are **synthetic** materials.

This cotton will be picked to be made into cloth.

Many clothes are made from cotton and polyester. The labels inside your clothes tell you what materials they are made of.

# Recycling

Materials cost money to make. Some materials can be **recycled** and used again. Which materials go in these recycling bins? (Answers on page 31.)

Plastic bottles can be recycled and made into clothes such as this fleece.

Most plastic cannot be recycled. Throwing plastic things away causes problems because plastic does not **rot** or rust. Plastic garbage lasts for a long, long time.

# Glossary

**flexible**  able to bend without breaking

**knitted**  threads looped together to make a cloth

**molten**  melted

**mold**  shape that can be filled with liquid. When the liquid hardens, it makes the same shape as the mold.

**natural**  comes from plants or animals, or found in the ground

**polished**  rubbed in order to make shiny

**pulp**  material that has been squashed and mixed with liquid

**precious**  very valuable

**rare**  not very common

**recycle**  use again

**rot**  become weak and crumbly

**spun**  twisted into a long thread

**synthetic**  not natural, made by people

**treat**  protect something using special chemicals

**waterproof**  keeps water out

# Answers

**Page 15**—Sapphires are blue.

**Page 25**—The plastic bag can be folded. The straps of the sandals, the green file, and the drinking straw can probably be folded, too.

**Page 28**—Plastic bottles, newspapers and magazines, glass bottles, and aluminum cans go in the recycling bins.

# More Books to Read

Oxlade, Chris. *How We Use Plastic.* Chicago: Heinemann Library, 2004.

Oxlade, Chris. *Wood.* Chicago: Heinemann Library, 2002.

# Index